CHARLES ROBINSON

THE FOUR GARDENS 1912

CHARLES

ALICE'S ADVENTURES IN WONDERLAND 1907

by Leo de Freitas
ROBINSON

ACADEMY EDITIONS · LONDON
ST. MARTINS PRESS · NEW YORK

To Patsy

Acknowledgements

The author wishes to express his thanks and gratitude for the assistance and encouragement given him by Miss Bay Robinson, Mr. Charles Robinson, Mr. Geoffrey Robinson and Mr. Ian Jeffrey. He would also like to take this opportunity of thanking the numerous book collectors and librarians who have made their collections freely available to him throughout his research, and in particular to Mr. George Fleming and Mr. Ian Hodgkins. To all he is indebted.
Special thanks are due to Graham Ovenden for permission to reproduce the majority of illustrations in this book from his extensive collection of Victorian illustrated books.

First published in Great Britain in 1976 by
Academy Editions 7 Holland Street London W8

SBN cloth 85670 277 3   SBN paper 85670 282 X

Copyright © Academy Editions 1976. All rights reserved

First published in the USA in 1976 by
St. Martin's Press Inc 175 Fifth Avenue, New York NY 10010

Library of Congress Catalog Card Number 76-11424

Reproduced and printed by photolithography and bound in Great Britain at The Pitman Press, Bath

Front cover illustration: THE BIG BOOK OF FABLES 1912

Back cover illustration: THE BIG BOOK OF NURSERY RHYMES 1903

THE BIG BOOK OF NURSERY RHYMES 1903

THE COLOUR PLATES

LILLIPUT LYRICS 1898 *17*

THE BIG BOOK OF NURSERY RHYMES 1903 *18*

THE SENSITIVE PLANT 1911 *35*

THE SENSITIVE PLANT 1911 *36*

THE HAPPY PRINCE 1913 *53*

THE HAPPY PRINCE 1913 *54*

THE SONGS AND SONNETS OF WILLIAM SHAKESPEARE 1915 *71*

THE SONGS AND SONNETS OF WILLIAM SHAKESPEARE 1915 *72*

Preceding page: SONGS OF INNOCENCE 1912

ONCE ON A TIME 1925

One day in March 1898 '. . . a very young unkempt pale nervous man with tremulous eyes' was invited, with the editor of *The Morning Post,* to lunch with the novelist and journalist Arnold Bennett. In his diary Bennett noted, 'One could see that not long since he had been more nervous than he is today. Contact with the world was making him less like a startled faun'. (1) Bennett would no doubt have been surprised to learn that he was just three years older than his 'very young' guest, but then Charles Robinson's character impressed upon everyone the idea that he was young. A short, slightly built man, with a characteristic jaunty walk, Robinson retained throughout his life that quality, so delightfully identified by Bennett, of being a 'startled faun'.

Charles Robinson was born the second child in a large family of four brothers and two sisters to Thomas and Eliza Robinson, in the borough of Islington, London, on October 22nd 1870. Unlike his elder brother Thomas, and his better known younger brother William, he was not christened with his mother's maiden name, Heath, but named after his father's brother, and closest friend, Charles.

For two generations prior to the younger Charles' birth the Robinson family had been associated with the pictorial press both as artists and craftsmen. His grandfather was in turn a bookbinder and then wood-engraver. Born in Newcastle upon Tyne, he travelled south to London to make a livelihood engraving for the growing number of illustrated newspapers and magazines: *Punch* and *The Illustrated London News* both appeared in the 1840s, and during the 1860s a number of other weekly illustrated papers emerged, such as *Good News, The Graphic* and *The Penny Illustrated Paper.* W. Heath Robinson mentions that his grandfather engraved the work of such distinguished artists and illustrators as George du Maurier, John Gilbert, Charles Green and Frederick Walker.

Charles' father and uncle both began their working lives in apprenticeships, and then made the transition to illustrating for the press. Thomas Robinson, the father of Charles, had been at first apprenticed to a watchmaker, at a later date took to wood-engraving, and finally chose to work as an illustrator. When his sons were born, and throughout their childhood, he was working for *The Penny Illustrated Paper*—affectionately called *The Pip*.

Charles Robinson, the uncle who was Robinson's namesake, served his time as an apprentice lithographic artist in the City of London firm of Maclure, Macdonald and Macgregor before leaving, shortly after his time expired, to take up illustrative journalism. During his apprenticeship he attended Finsbury School of Art, and in 1857, at the age of seventeen, he submitted work for the National Art Competition, organised by the Department of Science and Art to publicise the work being done in the State Art Schools throughout the country. Out of the thousands of original applicants, he was one of the final hundred to receive the coveted Silver Medal. It is quite possible that this early success helped him in securing a post on the staff of *The Illustrated London News*, which he retained for the remaining years of his short life.

Robinson's father had a studio near the newspaper and printing offices but he often worked at home, and it is only to be expected that his sons should have received their earliest training from him. Along with his brothers, Charles was able to watch the progress of his father's drawings, and one can imagine the kind of informal instruction passed down from the father to his sons as they set about copying the illustration on the drawing board. Had Charles Robinson's formative years been in any decade of the nineteenth century other than the '90s, it would probably have been possible to draw a comparison, based on continuities, between his work and that of his father. He was certainly well acquainted with the techniques used by both artists and craftsmen working on wood engravings, and was able to apply these techniques successfully whenever he felt them suitable. But the atmosphere of that last decade demanded new styles and ideas from aspiring young artists, and the different restrictions imposed upon them by the new processes by which their work would be reproduced required an original approach.

Unlike his brothers, Charles was never able to attend art schools on a full time basis. After a secondary education at the Old Islington High School, he was a student, for only a brief period, at the Highbury School of Art before having to sign apprenticeship indentures with the printers, Waterlow and Son. Like his uncle, he served his time as a lithographic artist working, in those days, directly on the large stones laid out in the printing shop. His 'Master' was George Sidney Waterlow, and it is likely that Robinson worked with him at the Finsbury branch of the firm which was under his management at that time. Throughout the seven years of his apprenticeship, Robinson attended art schools as an evening student, and then in July 1892 he was admitted as a Probationer at the Royal Academy, becoming enrolled on the Register of Students less than one month later. However, the ill luck, in the form of inadequate finances, which had dogged any chance of a full time art education in the past, intervened again and forced him to abandon studies at the Academy Schools. Continuing to attend classes in the evening, he studied at the West London School of Art, and at the internationally famous Heatherleys—where, incidentally, he was following in the path of such illustrators as George Pinwell, Frederick Walker, Walter Crane and

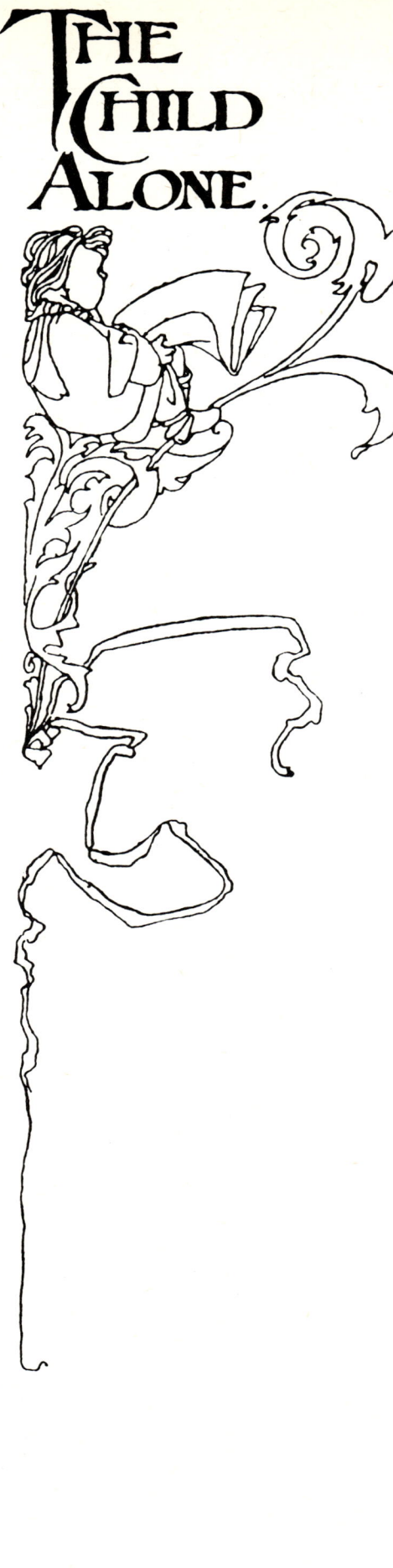

RAIN

The rain is raining all around,
It falls on field and tree,
It rains on the umbrellas here,
And on the ships at sea.

Phil May

Robinson was always conscious of never having benefited from a full time art education. In his autobiography, W. Heath Robinson made the following comments on his brother's lack of formal training, and his subsequent approach to illustration: 'In the long run this handicap, if such it was, does not seem to have affected his work. Whether he would have benefited from a more academic training it would be difficult to say. Perhaps it would have checked his delightful freedom and his most original fancy.' (2)

From the end of his apprenticeship to the year 1895 Robinson put together a portfolio of work from which to make his living. His first sale likely to have been of any career value appears to have been made to Joseph Darton of the publishing firm Wells, Gardner, Darton and Company. It was illustrative of one of his father's nonsense rhymes. It would be tempting to claim that from this, his very earliest sale, he was a wholly fantastical artist drawing on the powers of his own imagination, but he was at the same time also working on architectural drawings, newspaper advertisements, work for the Society for Promoting Christian Knowledge, and illustrations for the children's magazines of Marcus Ward, Cassell and others.

Throughout this period he was working alongside his brother Tom at their father's studio—two rooms at the top of Number One, Danes Inn, The Strand. It was remembered and described by Will Heath Robinson as a place '. . . approached by a very wide circular stairway with an iron railing to deter anyone so disposed from throwing themselves on to the pavement below. A stale smell of old dinners pervaded the place and belied the otherwise prison-like character of the building.' (3)

The young Charles Robinson, along with his brothers, found the Bohemian life-style peculiar to Fleet Street in the 1890s a stimulating one. Many of the men he admired, and who eventually became his friends, worked as illustrators for the flourishing pictorial press, and an unsigned drawing of his is to be found in the famous album kept by the Cheshire Cheese Tavern, alongside the signatures of Phil May, Cecil Aldin, Tom Browne, F.C. Gould and Harry Furniss. Considering the rural wholesomeness and idyllic tranquillity of gardens which characterise the majority of his drawings, it is difficult to imagine them starting to form in his mind whilst he worked in the claustrophobic surroundings of his father's studio, and in the smokey, noisy atmosphere of the Fleet Street inns.

The year 1895 was to be a year of opportunity and undoubted success for the young artist. The first of his drawings appeared in the February 16th number of the magazine *Black and White*. They illustrate a light-hearted story of Valentines by S. Squire Sprigge, and in style and technique are the complete opposite of one another. The first, a half-tone reproduction of a wash drawing, is purely illustrative of the text, there being no attempt made at *decorating* the drawing in any way. Although it is a competent illustration, nothing distinguishes it from any one of the thousands of like drawings appearing in the pictorial press and illustrated books at that time. The second one, however, is rather more interesting and revealing. Robinson was only one of a number of artists who parodied Aubrey Beardsley's exuberant style, and this tongue-in-cheek illustration is quite in keeping with the frivolous way in which, friend and foe alike, illustrators reacted to Beardsley's work. With the impish irreverence set to one side, the drawing suggests a sympathy with the decorative use of line which Robinson came to master so well. Every young artist was affected by Beardsley's approach to illustration, and Robinson, before taking his own path, part repaid his debt by teasing the Teaser. Although he was to use Beardsleyesque conventions on occasions throughout his black and white line work, the only other *imitations* of Beardsley he did were in a series of Christmas cards, menu cards and programmes commissioned by Marcus Ward and Company (*The Artist*, reviewing these Christmas cards commented: '. . . if they are not by Aubrey Beardsley, [they] very well might be'). At a later date (probably 1896) these were

THE CHILD WORLD 1896

brought together in a yellow bound booklet and, with a text written by Robinson, were published as *Christmas Dreams,* by Awfly Weirdly.

In March a full-page line illustration decorating a poem by Blanche Lindsay appeared in *Black and White*, and then in April three little books in the Macmillan's New Literary Readers Series were published with his illustrations. Although delightful little books in themselves, and worthy of more attention, their importance here lies in their being reviewed, with a reproduction of one of the drawings, in *The Studio* magazine. In this brief review a wider audience was introduced to the Charles Robinson child, and promised a longer illustrated paper on the 'clever young artist'.

In the early months of the year Robinson had submitted work for the Metropolitan Sketch Clubs' Competition. Two of his drawings won firsts: 'Life in Fairyland' (later to be reproduced in *Make Believe,* 1896) taking the prize for figures, and 'A Bible Illustration' the prize for design. Both of these drawings, plus a sketch for a stained glass panel and an illustration, 'The Children with Rabbits', to a fairy tale of his own, were reproduced in *The Studio* article. Published the month following his first notice, this article was most encouraging, praising not only his original expression of humour, but also his style as a decorative artist. Whilst mildly rebuking him for using Gothic script on an already ornate illustration, the reviewer generally chose to applaud and encourage: 'The individuality of these drawings promises a good deal, and if Mr. Robinson, who seems so far to have escaped the influence of three of his contemporaries to quite a remarkable degree, and to be neither Charles Ricketts, R. Anning Bell nor Aubrey Beardsley, but himself, will go on in the same path, one may expect a personal style that will take a far higher place than the exercises in the style of the three clever designers whose names I have quoted.' (4)

Although *The Studio* article must have been of undoubted value to him, it was indirectly, through its editor, that the magazine really contributed to Robinson's first major commission, and by way of its acclaim, to his almost overnight success. A Mr. Charles Baxter, friend and executor of Robert Louis Stevenson who had died the previous year (1894), offered to John Lane the rights to publish an illustrated version of Stevenson's *A Child's Garden of Verses*, first published in 1885. Looking for a suitable artist, Lane turned to his friend Charles Holme, then the editor of *The Studio*, who introduced him to the work of a selected number of young illustrators. As soon as the publisher saw Robinson's work he was convinced that this was the man who could best interpret the poet's collection of verses. Speed was essential, and within days Robinson found himself with a contract not only to illustrate the poems, but also to design the layout and presentation of the book—this all to be completed in time for the Christmas book lists.

At the age of twenty-five, Robinson joined the band of extremely talented young artists drawn together by John Lane to work for the Bodley Head publishing firm. Among others connected with the young publishers at that time were Walter Crane, Henry James, Selwyn Image, Kenneth Grahame, Aubrey Beardsley, Edmund Gosse and Wilfrid Meynell—some among the many—and it is certain that Robinson shared in their company at the smoking parties and tea parties held by Lane.

The second half of the year must have been a busy and possibly anxious time for Robinson. In addition to the Stevenson book, he had accepted commissions for frontispiece and title-page designs for a number of other works, and a commission to illustrate a small edition of *Aesop's Fables* in Dent's Banbury Cross Series. In the month that *A Child's Garden of Verses* was published, three more of his drawings were reproduced in *Black and White*, two appearing in the special Christmas number.

In December 1895 John Lane published the first illustrated edition of Stevenson's collection of poems, and it can be assumed that from its immediate success he must have been more than satisfied with his choice

GARDEN DAYS.

MAKE BELIEVE 1896

of illustrator. *The Studio*, in undisguised pleasure at *their* protégé's success, commented: '. . . The artist has acquitted himself magnificently of his task, and we take especial pleasure in recording his success. Everyone who likes prettily decorated books should buy this little work.' (5)

Generally the book reviewers in the United States of America, as well as in Britain, were of the opinion that the young, and hitherto unknown, artist, with his gifts of delicate draughtsmanship and thoughtful design, combined with a light-hearted, yet perceptive, understanding of children and their worlds, was certainly deserving of the acclaim he was sure to receive. *The Bookman*, an illustrated literary journal published in New York, first queried: '. . . Has he illustrated Stevenson? There may be two opinions about that.' But then went on encouragingly: 'But he has depicted childhood in all its remoteness from the grown-up land, in its heroic and fantastic imaginings, in its long thoughts and its short sight. . . Poet and artist meet and part in an interesting fashion. And it is not merely as a book of graceful pictures that this one which Mr. Robinson has done so much to make beautiful will be treasured. It is Stevenson's exquisite Child's Garden with still more childhood put into it.' (6)

Lane, the entrepreneur of collectors' limited editions, published one hundred and fifty signed copies with the edition for general release, and although the work was reprinted many times up until 1952 it is to these original editions that one must turn to appreciate Robinson's early illustrative and design capabilities. Subsequent editions appeared in different sizes, generally smaller, and it is not an exaggeration to say that, outside the format in which the illustrations were conceived, many of the designs lose their appeal. Drawings forfeit the balance between printed and unprinted areas on the pages, and head and tail pieces can become mere decoration, when once they satisfied the dual functions of interpretation and decoration.

From the success of *A Child's Garden of Verses* Robinson went on to illustrate well over one hundred books. The majority were children's books, and in many of them the fearless Charles Robinson child, with his thick wavy hair and rustic clothes, encountered by many for the first time gambolling his way through Stevenson's poems, is to be found somewhere. As sophisticated, young, Aesthetic ladies and gentlemen typified Kate Greenaway's work, and Arthur Rackham became inseparable from his wizened elves and dwarfs, so the public expected of Charles Robinson his graphic evocation of childhood played out by the innocent, and not so innocent, characters who ran riot, or just dallied, across the 'Land of Counterpane', and 'Up the Mountainside of Dreams'.

As *A Child's Garden of Verses* launched Robinson on his career as a successful and popular illustrator, so

its publication has to be associated with the decision of the artist and Edith Mary Favatt to marry. On the royalties from the book, and the prospects suggested for the future from its wide acclaim, they were married in April 1897. Charles was twenty-six and Edith twenty-one. Among the many guests were John Lane, Walter Jerrold, H.D. Lowry, Evelyn Sharp and the Reverend Percy Dearmer—the last named marrying the young couple. Their first home was in West End Lane, Hampstead, and Edith, although not an artist herself, came to be a continual source of support and encouragement to Charles throughout his life; her approval of a drawing or a painting was as important to him as the comments from fellow artists. Their immediate future looked, and indeed proved to be, prosperous enough, but there were to be less secure times in the fast approaching new, and unknown, century. With a large family to support, and the problem of dwindling commissions due to a decline in demand for the lavishly illustrated book just before the First World War, Charles' optimism and trust in the future were bound to be severely taxed, and during these times one can readily appreciate how much he must have valued Edith's understanding and patient nature.

Opportunities particular to the last decade of the nineteenth century gave scope to artists inclined towards treating the book as something more than just a utilitarian object. Some illustrators were content to do no more than represent the facts in the author's text without venturing beyond, as closely as possible, a photographic exactness. But there were many who energetically devoted themselves towards perfecting a union between illustration and decorative ideals, with textural embellishments and inventive composition and design. Robinson's work was never associated with any other style than that of the decorative artists (although, exceptionally, he produced work of a purely pictorial nature), and Brian Doyle in his *Who's Who in Children's Literature,* generously ascribes to Robinson the title of *decorative artist par excellence,* claiming: '. . . No one has excelled his intricate flower-and-baby-entwined title pages, chapter headings and illustrations.' (7)

As a largely self-schooled illustrator and designer in the 1890s, he was from the beginning influenced by the decorative aesthetic which had evolved out of the writings of John Ruskin, the work of the Pre-Raphaelite artists, and William Morris and the Arts and Crafts Movement. In book design the decorative artists were naturally closely wedded to the concept of the *Book Beautiful,* and when Robinson found himself in the role of book designer, a role he enjoyed and fulfilled comfortably, he showed a knowledge of, and fidelity to, ideals basically taken from the principles of book decoration and arrangement suggested by

MAKE BELIEVE 1896

Walter Crane. Crane's Cantor Lectures on Decorative Illustration, given before the Society of Arts in 1889, were first published in book form in 1896, although Robinson was familiar with Crane's ideas when he illustrated and designed *A Child's Garden of Verses.*

The book was to be seen as an integrated whole and, as such, it was as wrong to ignore the relationship of the binding material, cover design, end-papers, and other 'preliminary' elements to one another and the rest of the book, as it was thoughtlessly to arrange illustrations without considering the format of the book or the type face with which they would be printed. Crane's altogether poetic discourse on general principles would have been of great appeal to Robinson who, undoubtedly, endorsed the author's suggestions that, in any illustrated book, the preliminary material—end-papers, fly-leaves, and half title-page—should be suggestive of what was in store, secretive and a little playful, so that the reader was to pass on with bated breath until his initial excitement was complete with the splendour of a beautifully designed title-page.

In nearly all his children's books (but especially is this true of the large and luxurious Christmas Gift books) Robinson applied this principle of visual surprise. Whether or not, in more sober post-Christmas moments, children appreciated that these designs were intended to whet their appetites, and obediently started at the covers and worked their way through, these thoughtful arrangements are indicative of the time and consideration he put into his designs. The same applies to the attention he paid to the size and arrangement of the illustrations within the text. The most useful way of fully appreciating this is to compare, where possible, two editions of a work in which the format of the book has been altered, but where the size of the illustrations and the type face have remained unchanged. One such example is Lewis Carroll's *Alice's Adventures in Wonderland,* first published with Robinson's illustrations in 1907, the year in which copyright protection on the story lapsed, and subsequently reprinted in a different format in 1913. Incidentally, Robinson's *Alice* was the first to have short hair, trespassing a tradition of waist length wavy hair set by John Tenniel. A photograph of Alice Liddell taken by Carroll in 1859 when she was seven, and originally pasted into his manuscript of *Alice's Adventures Under Ground* as a tail-piece, shows her with bobbed hair, and a similar photograph of her, taken at about the same age, was reproduced in *The Strand Magazine* in 1898. It is quite possible that Robinson knew of this portrait, and that it suggested to him the idea of drawing his Alice in close resemblance to the 'original'—a decision which, apparently, caused a gentlemanly confrontation between artist and publisher!

Not only has it been reduced in size (although by only a matter of millimetres) with the result that illustrations and text are ill-fitting parts, but it has also completely lost the character of the gift book edition of 1907. The first edition's blue cloth cover, with its design in gold leaf, shows off the book in a very delicate and refined way, whereas the printed coloured cover of the 1913 version is, in comparison, crude and far less attractive. Although the cover design of the later edition is taken from one of the illustrations reproduced in the text, one cannot help but believe that Robinson had nothing to do with the designing and presentation of this reprint. The emptiness of the preliminary pages and the plainness of the title-page of the 1913 edition give the book an air of compromise—of being acceptable, but lacking any enthusiastic invitation to be handled and read. The fault must lie entirely with the publisher, as the 1907 edition is the true testament of the artist's intentions.

As a designer of decorative book covers, Robinson produced some fine examples in the children's gift books. In the nineteenth century the idea of decorating covers with the intention of increasing sales seems generally to have come before the claim for artistically designed covers as an indispensable part of the *Book Beautiful.* At their best these two approaches combined to provide us with some superb works of book art, although this did not begin to happen until responsibility for the design shifted from the printer or book-binder to the publisher, and through him to the illustrator.

KING LONGBEARD 1898

AT THE GATE OF DREAMLAND.

The Infant books designed and illustrated by Robinson throughout the first decade of the twentieth century were invariably bound in card or a stiff paper cover, giving the designer little scope. It is probable that these little books were seen to be expendable, and it is to the more substantial publications—the gift books and Classics—that one must look to find the best of his work. For those books considered special, by far the favourite materials appear to have been gold leaf and a good quality cloth. The richly illustrated Christmas gift books, such as *The Big Book of Fairy Tales, The Big Book of Nursery Rhymes* and *The Big Book of Fables,* were nearly always bound in red cloth with a very intricate design blocked on in gold leaf. His cover designs for these books always varied, and a composition was never repeated. Their sumptuousness was part of the extravagance of Christmas, as much so as visits to the pantomime, or the large family reunions, and the brilliance of their cloth and opulence of their gold designs were intended to express the light-heartedness and sense of well-being of the season.

Gold leaf on cloth was often used on the smaller gift books such as *King Long Beard, The Fairies' Fountain* and *The Cloud Kingdom,* and once or twice Robinson employed it on leather binding, as in *The Fireside Saints.* Occasionally he chose to have the design printed in one or two colours on the cloth, an example of which is the cover of *The Vanishing Princess,* where the figure in white, and the lettering in black, are printed onto a blue cloth. Covers were also printed in multiple colours, for example, the Art Nouveau inspired designs to *Anderson's Fairy Tales, The Suitors of Aprille* and *Pierette.*

Robinson designed the covers not only of works to which he contributed illustrations, but also of non-illustrated books where the publishers wanted attractively decorated covers. Alice Meynell's *The Children,* and one edition of Kenneth Grahame's *The Golden Age,* are examples of such work, as is Arnold Bennett's *Journalism for Women.* It was during Robinson's visit to Bennett that he mentioned having been offered commissions for some twenty cover designs due to the success of the *Journalism for Women* cover.

The spine design of a book is equally important as the design on the cover, if not more so, and Robinson's ornate treatment of the spine, generally filling up the area visible to the eye with lettering, flowing line work and often a miniature, made his books prominent on the shelves, and at no cost to the clarity of the author and title statements.

He remained faithful to the ideal of the book as a harmonious entity throughout his illustrative career and if, once or twice, he appears to have forsaken it, the explanation will undoubtedly be found either in the commercial economies forced upon designers or the possibility of his having acted as illustrator only.

Unfortunately, the many sketches and drafts of cover designs, end-papers and page arrangements drawn up by him for publishers, plus the hand made 'dummies', have almost all been lost, and in consequence his work as it appeared in published form has to act as evidence of the dedication he felt to the *Book Beautiful.*

Decorative book artists were encouraged to look back to the fifteenth and sixteenth centuries for inspiration and examples of how to approach the ornamentation of books. Crane continually urged artists and designers to devote time to the study of the early printed books, emphasising the crucial lessons of balance, or harmony, to be found in them as well as good examples of refined and fitting page decoration. *Early Venetian Printing Illustrated* (1895), with examples of calligraphy and ornate work applicable to book decoration, was one of the books Robinson kept in his studio, and from the excellent lettering he was able to produce, plus the fine scroll work to be found in various borders and headings in both books and magazines, it can be inferred that it was not often left idle. The decoration of the title pages of many of his earlier books, the rich border designs with their repeating foliage elements, and finely wrought pen-work reminiscent of illuminated manuscripts and incunabula, all plainly show his initial interest in these early examples of book and page decoration.

A perhaps more obvious, and certainly more important source of influence on his illustrative development, was the work of Albrecht Dürer. Throughout the nineteenth century Dürer's work was made more available to the public in Britain through facsimile reproductions, and Robinson owned a number of the books on Dürer and his work, including the *Literary Remains of Albrecht Dürer* (1889), a work documenting the growth of the artist's ideas

"Up the mountain sides of dreams."

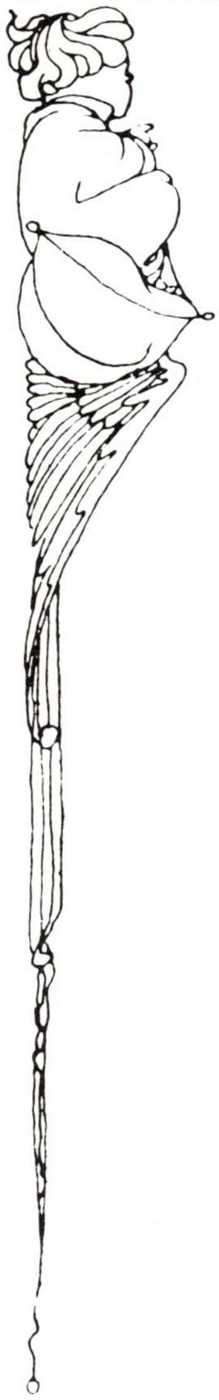

The moon has a face like the clock in the hall;

A CHILD'S GARDEN OF VERSES 1895

THE TRUE ANNALS OF FAIRYLAND: THE REIGN OF KING HERLA 1900

about art, and including his four books on human proportion. Illustrations from *The Small Passion* were mounted and hung in Robinson's studio and along the hall of his house. Robinson clearly admired Dürer's precise draughtsmanship and fidelity to nature. Successful line drawing demands skill in observation and selection, and is probably the most exacting of mediums. There can be little ambiguity in drawing in line: if an artist's work is good it says so and if it is less than this it expresses it likewise. Dürer, as a master in the technique of line drawing, was afforded a great amount of respect by Robinson.

Although Robinson's full page illustrations to poems published in the *Black and White Magazine* exhibit a blend of Düreresque and Pre-Raphaelite styles in their mediaevalism and attention to natural detail, there were a number of specific characteristics that he adopted from the master and used often in his early work. The radiant sun throwing closely woven beams almost to the edge of the drawing from a brilliant central orb appears quite consistently, and a number of his miniature landscapes suggest Dürer's Tyrolean countryside, with the ubiquitous river meandering its way through the valleys. Outcrops of rock with fortified burgs or castles springing from them occasionally find their way from mediaeval wood-cuts to Robinson's illustrations to fairy tales or poems, and in these illustrations it is often possible to detect the influence of Dürer in the lack of a middle distance. Then there are the fantastic towns and hamlets. Modelled on the Gothic architecture he found in Dürer's work, these make-believe communities became an indispensable part of Robinson's fairyland. Whether spied upon from the topmost branches of trees, or more often from clouds, or from across a valley, or again from the bottom of a hill, the crooked and rambling towns, with their spiked and turreted cathedrals and castles, became very much a symbol of the child's world. With a full moon throwing foreboding shadows across walls and along streets, what child's imagination would not thrill at the thought of strange and far away places with the chance of meeting such fabulous people as Old King Cole or coming face to face with fearsome characters like the Wee Men or Trolls? These townscapes owe a lot to Dürer, and yet they are timeless. Through Dürer's drawings we can come to understand a little of the environs about the artist, but in Robinson's use of the Gothic we are steeped in a part of an enchanted land of no fixed time or place in history. The decoration on entablatures and arches, in stained glass windows and in other decorative elements of buildings, the exaggerated towers and winding cobbled streets impart no sense of period, for they are selected facets which have become part of the symbolism of fairyland—timeless and enduring.

Robinson was also an admirer of the, then, newly rediscovered *quattrocento* artists, Botticelli and Filippino Lippi, as well as the Renaissance artists Leonardo, Michelangelo and Raphael. In this he shared in the enthusiasm of his time. Ruskin, the Pre-Raphaelites, and still later members of the Aesthetic Movement, acclaimed the work of Botticelli, and it is likely that Robinson came to know the early Italian masters through his appreciation of this research. In his personal collection of books he owned Giovanni Morelli's two-volumed *Italian Masters* (1892).

One might tentatively suggest that the influence of these artists can be seen in the serene facial expressions of many of Robinson's female studies, and especially the religious ones, the care with which he draped the human figure in loose flowing materials, and the occasional use of Italian architectural details. However, if he admired them, this did not prevent an impish humour, shared by all three brothers, from tweaking their leonine tails. In a series of paintings entitled 'Art Antics' he painted parodies of the great artists' work, selecting just those essential qualities of the individual styles with which to characterise them accurately. In one painting, Botticelli's 'Primavera' is adapted to the reporting of a girls' hockey match, and in another, one of Rembrandt's burghers nervously and tearfully contemplates a measel on his nose, fading into the sombre shadows of ink washes.

THE TRUE ANNALS OF FAIRYLAND: THE REIGN OF KING HERLA 1900

As might be expected, Robinson was an admirer of Japanese prints and drawings. There remains of his collection six paper-bound books of black and white and coloured wood engravings, and one large tome *Artistic Japan: Illustrations and Essays* (1891). Since the 1860s and 1870s, Japanese 'objets d'art' had been a source of inspiration to artists. Exotic plants and blossoms, besides the Japanese fan and screen, began to appear in the paintings of the avant garde, and the example of spatial harmony to be found in Japanese prints began to influence compositional treatment. In the graphic arts there were those able and willing to appreciate the sophistication of the Far East. Walter Crane, for example, records that of the various sources of influence on his own books for children, it was a collection of Japanese pictures which '... gave me the real impulse to that treatment in strong outlines, and flat tints and solid blacks, which I adopted with variations in books of this kind from that time (about 1870) onwards.' (8)

Robinson seems to have profited from the example of the Japanese illustrators, and it is the careful balance of black and white masses which so readily suggests their presence in his work. The superb draughtsmanship of Japanese illustrators must surely have been of great delight to him, and yet there is another facet of Japanese art which was likely to have been of even more immediate pleasure. Master draughtsmen, such as Hokusai, found a rich source of illustrative material in the everyday events of people around them, and it is this anecdotal element in their work which one feels certain Robinson appreciated. The dilemma of demure young ladies caught in the blast of wind which has succeeded in turning their parasols inside out whilst at the same time lifting their kimonos; the incidents of minor importance, such as the tying of a sandal by a porter, or of another wiping his brow, given almost equal status to Mount Fuji, the central theme of the print; and the deftly drawn expressions of awe, bashfulness, fear, anger or incredulity on the faces of characters, whether major or minor, are examples of the kind of observations which must have fascinated Robinson.

This ability of his to capture the minor, but far from insignificant, act or expression was the quality most welcomed by the reviewers and critics of his early work. The child observed trying to outwit his own shadow, or stalking the gardener with a pop gun, or again found tucked up in bed with a watering can, in fact any one of the numerous ways in which they appear throughout his books show how much the Japanese artists had guided his eye as well as his hand.

The 1890s also saw the acceleration of the application to printing of photomechanical processes. This had important consequences for artists. Although it had a fundamental effect on their approach to graphic work it is often played down in favour of the more exotic and stylistic impact of the Art Nouveau. To overestimate the latter at a cost of diminishing the significance of the new methods by which artists' originals were reproduced is to fall a prey to what Percy Muir amusingly calls the 'Art Nouveau Flapdoodle.' (9)

From the earliest days of photography, photomechanical means of reproducing illustrations had been sought, but 'process work', the generic term for the numerous printing methods utilising photography, did not become established until the 1880s. The first commercially viable step was the photomechanical line-block. The earliest examples of this process were generally rather poor, and the degradation of illustrative art at its hands was all grist to the mill of the critics of mass-production methods; William Morris, in particular, abhorred the shoddiness of industrial production. However, these poor reproductions were due rather to the teething troubles in the change over from wood engraved blocks to printing plates produced with the aid of photography than to anything inherently amiss with machine production. The technical problems were only slowly solved, largely because of the organisational problems of running photographically orientated printing works, but by the middle of the last decade publishers were able to take full advantage of this cheaper method of reproducing black

THE TRUE ANNALS OF FAIRYLAND: THE REIGN OF KING HERLA 1900

THE TRUE ANNALS OF FAIRYLAND: THE REIGN OF KING HERLA 1900

and white illustrations.

The major claim made in favour of the process methods was that, from the artist's point of view, his original drawings were reproduced *exactly* as he had drawn them, and not as some intermediary—the wood engraver—had interpreted them. Instead of drawing his work onto a woodblock, as his father and uncle had done, Robinson drew his work on white paper or card. Photographs of the drawings were then printed onto metal plates, specially prepared with light sensitive surfaces, and finally etched in acid baths which left the design in relief ready to be printed with the text. It will be understood that this process could only reproduce an illustration drawn in black and white much like the wood engravings which hitherto had appeared in books and magazines. One could legitimately ask what the benefits of this new process were for the artist when all that appeared to have happened was that the 'tyranny of the engraver' had been exchanged for the 'tyranny of the mechanical process' —the tail was still wagging the dog. However, providing illustrators understood the limitations of the process, and designed their work intelligently, the final result would be an exact facsimile of the original. For the first time it was possible for the artist's intentions, as expressed in his original work, to be faithfully reproduced without being modified by the engraver.

In a lecture delivered before the Society of Arts in 1895, entitled 'Drawing for Process Reproduction,' Gleeson White remarked: 'Instead of trying to raise illustration by retracing our steps, and trying to be imitative of the fifteenth century—endeavouring to make a system which sufficed for a simple civilisation work under quite new conditions—would it not be better logic to accept machine printing, shiny apper, the process engraver and his work, and by mastering these new conditions—as the artist most assuredly can master any conditions if he sets his mind to the effort— to create new ideas, and set up new standards of taste and beauty?' (10)

Charles Robinson certainly helped create new canons of taste and beauty in those active early years. His achievement rested just as much on the knowledge and skill he gained during his apprenticeship with the printers Waterlows as on his acquaintance with the work of Dürer or that of the Arts and Crafts workers. It was always important to him to know how things worked; he had something of the patience of the craftsman. He spent a good deal of time in understanding the three colour process of photomechanical reproduction, for example, and in *The Studio* of 1900 one of his watercolours, *The Norns*, was reproduced to show the potential of the new colour process. It is a singularly uncharacteristic example of his delicate watercolours, but it serves to illustrate his willingness to experiment and understand, to use and adapt to, the new processes.

Predictably, as Robinson's work passed into the twentieth century the presence of the early influences became less obvious. The very strong personal character evident in his earliest work asserts itself until it reaches a zenith in the black and white illustrations to A.A. Milne's *Once on a Time* (1925), and Winifred Radcliffe's *The Saint's Garden* (1927). Here, after more than thirty years of drawing, his illustrations are even more delicate, and less obviously derivative, than the best work of his younger years. There is a fluidity of line which is more relaxed and confident, and personal, and is seen at its clearest in his drawings of wild countryside flora and genteel gardens. Although his accumulated skill as a painter in watercolours may be in part accountable for this extraordinary delicacy of treatment in black and white, it must surely be a lifetime of drawing which offers the most satisfactory answer to the assurity of line and confidence of execution which these drawings exhibit. It is difficult to know what he could have done to improve upon this pen work, and this in itself might in part explain why the brush and pallet of the watercolour painter usurped the pen and ink of the draughtsman.

Charles Robinson became one of the most popular illustrators of children's literature during that prolific period spanning the transition from the nineteenth to the twentieth century. It is right that his work should be remembered for the high degree of care and craftsmanship which went into it, and yet it would be inadmissible to ignore what might be seen as the ephemeral books for infants. One has the impression that every nursery had its favoured collection of Robinson's infant books with their simple texts and illustrations. The small format of these books comfortably suited the hands that were to hold them, and the large, clear print plus the brightly coloured drawings suggest that they were designed to induce the child to

THE TRUE ANNALS OF FAIRYLAND:
THE REIGN OF OLD KING COLE 1900

want to read for himself rather than be read to. Both the drawings and the colouring of these books are vigorous, lacking the delicacy of treatment with which Robinson is usually associated, and the children within their pages are caricatures of the children to be found in his earliest work, with their chubby faces, masses of thick hair and infant dress. Other figures are drawn with the same simplicity of style and economy of line that he first employed in many of the illustrations to *Lilliput Lyrics* (1899), and in character Edward Lear's drawings suggest themselves as a source of inspiration for these creations. Although uncharacteristic of the bulk of his work, these illustrations are more modern in that they anticipate the simple forms to be found in many of the infant books of today. Their style suggests the atmosphere in which they were made. With his own young family around him, and those of his relations and friends, one can imagine the demands made on him to draw a soldier, sailor, a house or a submarine, and with the child on one knee, and a

THE SPOTTED MIMULUS.

THE CLOUD KINGDOM 1905

sketch book on the other, he would begin quick sketches for the child's amusement and education. At a later date, perhaps, these drawings might be worked up and coloured and, with a suitable text, turned into one of the 'Miniature Picture Books'.

However, if he was popular with a book buying public, and the majority of critics, this popularity did not endear him to every reviewer of illustrative literature. In an article entitled 'Concerning Children's Books', which appeared in *The Book of Book Plates* for 1903-04, the writer criticises Robinson for his illustrations to the *Big Book of Nursery Rhymes:* '... The illustrations are frankly disappointing, for all their scope, number, and elaboration. Mr. Robinson is too clever: he has all the facility that practise can give him; but he is mannered all through, and the mannerisms have taken the place of nature. The humour is that of exaggerated attitude, of distorted expression: not inherent humour at all—that is to say, Mr. Robinson's children are not children, but are drawn to a sort of recipe, which will draw you anything if but learned fairly...' (11) In support of these criticisms the reviewer contrasts *The Big Book of Nursery Rhymes* with Leslie Brooke's entertaining little book *Johnny Crow's Garden*. Brooke's illustrations really are humorous and original, although the choice of illustration reproduced in this article alongside an example of Robinson's work is not the best from the book. Robinson's drawing of a young girl clutching an umbrella and looking resignedly up into the sky as it begins to rain demonstrates the exaggerated attitude and distorted expression censured by the critic. It exhibits a hurriedness of execution in broken lines and lack of careful detail.

It would be wrong to ignore the criticism of mannerism evident in Robinson's work at this time, and even a criticism of inconsistency in some of his draughtsmanship, but the overstatement displayed in this review suggests quite wrongly that his imagination was exhausted and that his work was hackneyed throughout. For almost ten years Robinson had been successfully illustrating books for young children, and if stylistically his figure studies appeared to have been drawn 'to a sort of recipe' it had been a recipe well loved and in demand. Certainly, severe demands would have been made on his inventiveness, considering the thousands of drawings he must have prepared, but only occasionally is his work so predictable as to be boring. It is difficult to imagine any artist willingly changing his style when success had assured for him a following, and a livelihood.

A more serious complaint might have been justly made against the sketchiness of a number of the artist's drawings. To those who looked forward to Robinson's carefully delineated illustrations, the handful of hurried drawings in *The Big Book of Nursery Rhymes* must have been a disappointment. As the reviewer recognised, they suggested that the artist was 'over busy'. Unfortunately, throughout his review the writer betrayed a rather spiteful contempt for Charles Robinson's *success,* which must call into doubt the ostensibly dispassionate criticism of the artist's work: '... "One hundred drawings to be done by Tuesday fortnight" would keep a better artist awake o' nights and develop in him, towards the end, an uplifting inspiration in the region of excuse. But not so Mr. Robinson. Not for him the burning of bridges and ships. Not for him any qualms on his own account. Is he not reviewed favourably everywhere? Pleasantly also to his ears comes the clatter of publishers falling over each other in order to attain Charles Robinson.' (12)

There are, indeed, one or two books, and a small number of illustrations scattered throughout other works, that suffer from hurried treatment, but the reason lies in the amount of work Robinson had to produce, and not in any attitude of complacency or over-confidence brought on by his success in publishing. Charles Robinson never suffered from an inflated idea of his own importance.

Throughout his work there is a consistent element of robustness and light-heartedness. People, places and animals are nearly always healthy both physically and mentally and it is rare to find the artist suggesting a negative side of life. Certainly, there are often characters to be found alone and in silence, but the drawings usually convey a feeling of peace when the one reflecting is not harassed by any real problems or

THE SENSITIVE PLANT 1911

36 THE SENSITIVE PLANT 1911

THE BIG BOOK OF NURSERY RHYMES 1903

anguish. However, there are examples (and as exceptions they remain the more memorable) where the artist guardedly comments upon those moments in life when one is confronted with situations not lightly shrugged away. Probably the best known illustration of this kind is that in *The Secret Garden* (1911), where Mary, recently arrived at the large cheerless home of her uncle, is standing on the steps leading into a pond. A wintry garden trails listless tendrils about the steps and the gigantic urns at her back, and the plain, lonely child stares at her reflection with an air of sadness and melancholy. One or two of the illustrations and vignettes to *The Sensitive Plant* (1911), and *The Songs and Sonnets of William Shakespeare* (1915) offer further examples of this element in his work.

Admirers of Charles Robinson who might wish to read that he was an eccentric in one way or another are to be sadly disappointed. In common with his brothers, Tom and Will, he enjoyed the conventions and regularity of domestic life. He and Edith had a large family of six children—four girls and two boys. Naturally they suggested material for his illustrations and were often called upon to model for him. Bay Robinson, the eldest of his children, remembers modelling as Mary for his illustrations to Francis Hodgson Burnett's *The Secret Garden*. Unlike many artists who require an exclusive atmosphere in their studios in order to work, Robinson often had children playing and drawing at his feet whilst he worked, and this familiarity with their ways and expressions is ever present in his child studies.

He was a very gregarious man and would, without a doubt, have called himself a Bohemian. His conception of Bohemianism was not one where social conventions were cast aside, but rather the sense of brotherhood to be found in the artists' clubs and debating circles. Readers of William Heath Robinson's autobiography will know that Charles was one of the original signatories of the Frothfinder's Charter, but he was also a member, and past President, of the Highgate Thirty Club—'Founded 1902 for the discussion of Papers, Debates and Social Intercourse'—and of the better known London Sketch Club and the Savage Club, serving a term as President of the first named from 1926-27. One of the best impressions to be found of this particular Bohemianism is that in *The Savage Club: A Medley of History, Anecdote and Reminiscence*: 'Bohemianism is not a gipsy style of living, but a temperament; not a carelessness of dress or disregard of niceness at meal-times, but an atmosphere. . .'; 'Life in Bohemia—in any section of Bohemia—is not the whole of life, but only a small part of it. An interval, a diversion, a few hours recreation at most, "A moment's taste," as Omar says, "of sweetness at the well beside the waste".' And a

A STRANGE SIGHT

UPON St. Paul's steeple stands a tree,
As full of apples as may be;
The little boys of London Town,
They run with hooks and pull them down;
And then they run from hedge to hedge,
Until they come to London Bridge.

little sadly: '. . . A true Bohemian, it is feared, is often merry without whilst he is sad enough within.' (13)

Certainly Charles Robinson valued very highly the brotherhood of his fellow artists, and from the early years of his marriage, when the home at West Hampstead was always open to friends, until towards the end of his life when he moved out of London, he shared to the full in the camaraderie of the Clubs, and the confidence to be found in the company of his 'Brother Sketchers'.

Not surprisingly, Charles Robinson became friends with many of the authors he met through his work and social life. He could count Edmund Gosse and Percy Dearmer among his friends, and Katherine Tynan Hinkson presented him with a copy of her book, *A Little Book of XXIV Carols*, inscribed 'To Charles Robinson from his friend and admirer Katherine Tynan Hinkson. Christmas 1907'. But undoubtedly the closest friendship he shared was with Walter C. Jerrold, the grandson of Douglas W. Jerrold (author of *Mrs. Caudle's Curtain Lectures*, 1846). Walter Jerrold, who also used the pseudonym Walter Copeland, was a prolific writer as a journalist and editor, and although the circumstances under which he and Charles were introduced are not known, it is likely that they met through a publisher—possibly Blackie who published their first book *Nonsense! Nonsense!* (1902). Not only did this prove to be a very successful working partnership (they collaborated on well over twenty books), but it also led to a firm friendship which lasted until Jerrold's death in 1929. Charles, when sending a portrait of the author, painted by Charles Ward, to

ALICE'S ADVENTURES IN WONDERLAND

Thinking of little Alice

Jerrold's daughter Hebe, wrote: 'So, my dear child, I hope you feel that it is a good portrait. I know it is a good painting, and I hope you will accept it as a token of lasting memory of the best man I have ever known. Your affectionate, but down trodden uncle, Charles Robinson.' (14)

Born in 1865, Walter Jerrold was only five years older than Charles and, when the two friends started their own families, the children were often visiting one another and going out on 'treats'. A yearly visit to the Zoo in Regent's Park, and the parties at Christmas (portrayed so exactly in *The Child's Christmas*, 1906) were highlights in the lives of both families. The sense of occasion, with the excitement and gaiety, was captured by both artists in the many infant books which they prepared during the first decade of the twentieth century. The titles of the books themselves suggest the kind of events and special visits the children would have made: *The Farm Book, The Book of the Zoo, The Book of Sailors, The Book of Soldiers, The Toy Shop, The Sweet Shop* and *The Cake Shop*. However, both artist and author would probably have considered the three 'Big Books', *The Big Book of Fables, Fairy Tales* and *Nursery Rhymes*, to be their most successful joint efforts. Their satisfaction and pleasure in these books is delightfully expressed in the tailpiece to *The Big Book of Fables*, where Charles has depicted both of them presenting the book to the reader—Walter Jerrold sporting a monocle, and Charles a rather fashionable moustache.

It would be convenient to be able to say that the disruption of the First World War caused the slump in demand for the lavishly illustrated book. However, it would appear that this began sometime prior to 1914, although the war obviously accelerated the trend. Robinson appears to have been at his busiest around 1905 to 1906 (in the five year period 1905 to 1909 some thirty-nine books illustrated by him were published), and if there was only a slow decline in the number of books he illustrated in the immediate years before the war, 1914 saw the beginning of the end. After a brief revival in 1915, probably representing books already commissioned, nothing appeared until 1919, and thereafter only the occasional book until 1932 when he stopped illustrating books altogether.

The war years certainly created difficulties and hardships for him and his family. Money for completed work was delayed and, with very few commissions to be had, he was obliged to accept any work he could find. During the hostilities, being too old for the regular forces, he enrolled as a member of the Volunteer Training Corps—the forerunner of the Home Guard—and at its disbandment had reached the rank of Second Lieutenant. Like many of the artists who joined these reserve army units he was often amused, and not infrequently embarrassed, by the 'actions' they were expected to take seriously. On one occasion his unit was ordered to stop a tram on Highgate Hill and search the vehicle for spies and weapons! He appears not to have been amused by this incident, but one cannot help but wonder if Will Heath Robinson took advantage of his brother's first hand descriptions in drawing some of his illustrations to the less serious aspects of defeating the Boche. Charles' hand-drawn route maps and instruction books must have been some of the most beautifully executed pieces of army paraphernalia to come out of that war. Unfortunately, with time they have all been lost.

Like so many of the 'Black and White' men who had prospered before the war, Robinson found his fortunes almost totally reversed after 1919. However, he turned to the work which was offered by the illustrated magazines such as the *Graphic, Pan* and *Queen,* and gradually his position improved. As his family grew up and began their own adult lives he expressed the desire to move out into the country and, with the increasing opportunities afforded by the return of regular commissions, he and Edith left London for a cottage in Botley, Buckinghamshire. It was here that he spent the last years of his life, working on watercolours for magazines and commercial art firms, as well as for his own pleasure. His painting deserves greater attention and research than is possible here, and it will have to suffice to say that in watercolour, as in pen and ink, his fine work earned him the respect and admiration of his fellow artists. He exhibited at the Royal Academy, the Royal Institute of Painters in Watercolours, at the Walker Art Gallery in Liverpool, and at galleries in Glasgow and Bristol. In 1932 he was elected R.I., and his pleasure and pride in this distinction can only be understood in terms of an artist, consciously aware of early deficiences in academic training, who is finally recognised by a body for which he has the greatest respect.

On the 13th June 1937 Charles Robinson died unexpectedly at the age of sixty-six. His early death came as a shock to the family, and not least to his brothers, Tom and Will. Known collectively as 'The Three Musketeers', the brothers had shared throughout their lives a very keen friendship, and now suddenly one vital element had gone. Rivalry there certainly must have been between the trio, but of more significance is the respect and admiration in which they held one another and their work, which endured to the end.

In the light of this strong fraternal bond it is appropriate that the last word should come from them. In 1938, Will Heath Robinson wrote of his brother's death: '... It was unbelievable. He was always so alive with an irrepressible vitality, it seemed impossible it could cease. His life had been one of work and some

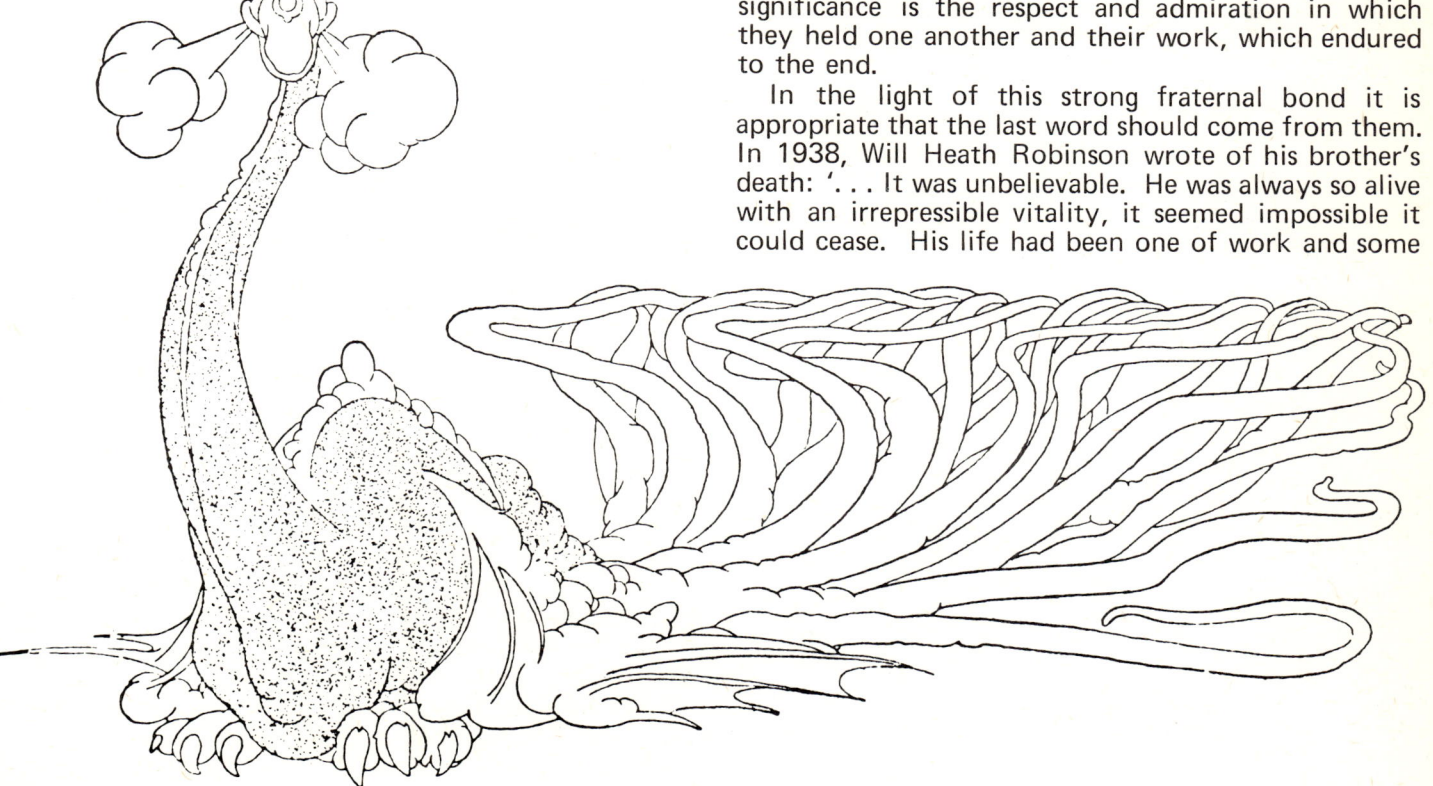

46 MAKE BELIEVE 1898

cease. His life had been one of work and some hardship. It had been a brave and successful struggle to be an artist and at the same time to bring up a large family. Yet there was always something of youth and of being on holiday about Charles. I went into his studio a few days before he died. Besides unfinished pictures, there was the incompleted model of a Spanish Galleon. It was already taking shape. Painted here and there with brilliant colour it gave promise of the proud and beautiful thing it was to have been. Although unfinished it was a triumph of the spirit over the years and the many vicissitudes of life that at last had laid him low. . .' And: 'Charles inherited his love for making ships from my father, whom he resembled in other ways. He was more concerned with his painting and his ship models than with theories about art. He was an artist first of all and last of all. He had the magic assistance so often given to genius. If he wanted to build a ship the materials somehow rose to his hands. As with his painting, it was all so easy and instinctive with him.' (15)

REFERENCES:

(1) BENNETT, A. *The Journals of Arnold Bennett: 1896-1910* Cassell (London, 1932)

(2) ROBINSON, W. HEATH *My Line of Life* Blackie (London, 1938)

(3) ibid.

(4) S., E.B. A New Book Illustrator: Charles Robinson *The Studio V* (1895) 146-150

(5) Book reviews *The Studio VI* (1895) 191-192

(6) Book reviews *The Bookman II* (New York, 1896)

(7) DOYLE, B. *The Who's Who of Children's Literature* Hugh Evelyn (London, 1968)

(8) CRANE, W. *Of the Decorative Illustration of Books Old and New* Bell (London, 1901)

(9) MUIR, P. *Victorian Illustrated Books* Batsford (London, 1971)

(10) WHITE, G. Drawing for process reproduction *Journal of the Society of Arts* 43 (1895) 277-291

(11) L. Concerning Children's Books *Books and book-plates* 4 (1903-04) 76-79

(12) ibid.

(13) WATSON, A. *The Savage Club: a Medley of History, Anecdote and Reminiscence* Unwin (London, 1907)

(14) Private source made available to the author

(15) ROBINSON, W. HEATH *My Line of Life* Blackie (London, 1938)

The Mouse gave a sudden leap out of the water

48 RICHARD WAGNER AND THE RING OF THE NIBELUNGS 1898

RICHARD WAGNER AND THE RING OF THE NIBELUNGS 1898

50 RICHARD WAGNER AND THE RING OF THE NIBELUNGS 1898

52 THE TRUE ANNALS OF FAIRYLAND: THE REIGN OF KING HERLA 1900

54 THE HAPPY PRINCE 1913

WINTER·HAS·COME

Cold and raw the north wind doth blow,
Bleak in a morning early;
All the hills are covered with snow,
And winter's now come fairly.

THE CLOUD KINGDOM 1905

60 THE CLOUD KINGDOM 1905

THE CLOUD KINGDOM 1905

There was a large pool all around her about four inches deep and reaching half down the hall

'Alice led the way and the whole party swam to the shore'

64 ALICE'S ADVENTURES IN WONDERLAND 1907

"When they take us up and throw us, with the lobsters, out to sea!"

THE SONGS AND SONNETS OF WILLIAM SHAKESPEARE 1915

BIBLIOGRAPHY

This bibliography is restricted either to books illustrated solely by Charles Robinson or to those where his work can be considered to have made a major contribution. Although, within these limits, the author would like to claim comprehensiveness he is aware that such a claim would be fatuous, and consequently, claims only that, to his knowledge, this bibliography is the nearest to a complete list of Robinson's work in book illustration to appear in print to date. The years of publication have been taken from the title pages of the books or, failing this from The English Catalogue and the British Museum Printed Catalogue. The dates of reprints are given only when significant changes have been made to Robinson's illustrations. The place of publication of all books is London unless otherwise stated.

It should be remembered, however, that Robinson designed in addition, an unknown number of covers, endpapers, frontispiece illustrations, headings, minor text illustrations and embellishments for many books and periodicals, as well as ephemera such as Christmas cards, book-plates and invitation cards.

The letters BW denote black and white illustrations and the letter C colour illustrations.

1895
AESOP'S FABLES (Dent)	BW
A CHILD'S GARDEN OF VERSES by R.L. Stevenson (Bodley Head)	BW
THE INFANT READER (Macmillan)	BW & C
THE FIRST PRIMER (Macmillan)	BW & C
THE SECOND PRIMER (Macmillan)	BW & C

ONCE ON A TIME 1925

BIBLIOGRAPHY

1896
ANIMALS IN WRONG PLACES by E. Carrington (Bell)	BW
THE CHILD WORLD by G. Setoun (Bodley Head)	BW
CHRISTMAS DREAMS by Awfly Weirdly (pseudonym: Charles Robinson) (Marcus Ward)	BW
MAKE BELIEVE by H.D. Lowry (Bodley Head)	BW
MINSTREL DICK by C.R. Coleridge (Gardner Darton)	BW

1897
DOBBIES' LITTLE MASTER by Mrs. A. Bell (Bell)	BW
LULLABY LAND by E. Field (Bodley Head)	BW

1898
KING LONGBEARD by B. Mac-Gregor (Bodley Head)	BW
LILLIPUT LYRICS by W.D. Rands (Bodley Head)	BW & C
RICHARD WAGNER & THE RING OF THE NIBELUNGS by L.N. Parker (Published for the Royal Opera Syndicate by Rudolph B. Bimbaum) Illustrated by C. Robinson and P. Billingshurst	BW

1899
FAIRY TALES FROM HANS CHRISTIAN ANDERSEN (Dent) Illustrated by Charles, Thomas and William Heath Robinson	BW
THE NEW NOAH'S ARK by J.J. Bell (Bodley Head)	C
PIERRETTE by H. de Vere Stacpool (Bodley Head)	BW
THE SUITORS OF APRILLE by N. Garstin (Bodley Head)	BW

1900
THE ADVENTURES OF ODYSSEUS by Homer (Dent)	BW & C
CHILD VOICES by W.E. Cule (Melrose)	BW
JACK OF ALL TRADES by J.J. Bell (Bodley Head)	C
THE LITTLE LIVES OF THE SAINTS by Rev. P. Dearmer (Wells, Gardner, Darton)	BW
THE MASTER MOSAIC-WORKERS G. Sand (Dent)	BW & C
SINTRAM AND HIS COMPANIONS by F.H.C. de la Motte Fouque (Dent)	BW & C
TALES OF PASSED TIMES by C. Perrault (Dent)	BW & C
THE TRUE ANNALS OF FAIRYLAND: THE REIGN OF KING HERLA Edited by W. Canton (Dent)	BW

1901
A BOOK OF DAYS FOR LITTLE ONES by C. Bridgman (Dent)	C
THE FARM BOOK by W. Copeland (Dent)	C
THE TRUE ANNALS OF FAIRYLAND: THE REIGN OF OLD KING COLE Edited by J.M. Gibbon (Dent)	BW

1902
THE BAIRNS CORONATION BOOK by C. Bridgman (Dent)	C
THE BOOK OF THE ZOO by W. Copeland (Dent)	C
THE CORONATION AUTOGRAPH BOOK (Wells, Gardner, Darton)	C
THE MOTHER'S BOOK OF SONG by J.H. Burn (Wells, Gardner, Darton)	BW
NONSENSE! NONSENSE! by W. Jerrold (Blackie)	C
THE SHOPPING DAY by C. Bridgman (Dent)	C
STORIES FOR CHILDREN by Charles & Mary Lamb (Dent) Illustrated by C. Robinson and W. Green	BW
THE TRUE ANNALS OF FAIRYLAND: THE REIGN OBERON Edited by W. Jerrold (Dent)	BW

BIBLIOGRAPHY

1903
THE BIG BOOK OF NURSERY RHYMES by W. Jerrold (Blackie) — BW & C
FIRESIDE SAINTS by D. Jerrold (Blackie) — BW & C
THE NEW TESTAMENT OF OUR LORD AND SAVIOUR JESUS CHRIST (Glasgow, Cowans & Gray) — BW

1904
SIEGFRIED by S. Baring Gould (Dean) — BW

1905
THE BLACK CAT BOOK by W. Copeland (Blackie) — C
A BOOKFUL OF FUN (Sealey Clark) — C
THE BOOK OF DUCKS AND DUTCHIES by W. Copeland (Blackie) — C
THE BOOK OF THE DUTCH DOLLS by W. Copeland (Blackie) — C
THE BOOK OF THE FAN by W. Copeland (Blackie) — BW & C
THE BOOK OF THE LITTLE DUTCH DOTS by W. Copeland (Blackie) — C
THE BOOK OF THE LITTLE J. Ds. by W. Copeland (Blackie) — BW & C
THE BOOK OF THE MANDARINFANTS by W. Copeland (Blackie) — BW & C
THE CLOUD KINGDOM by I.H. Wallis (Bodley Head) — BW
THE TEN LITTLE BABIES by C. Robinson (S.P.C.K.) — C

1906
AWFUL AIRSHIP by W. Copeland (Blackie) — C
BABY TOWN BALLADS by Netta (Sealey Clark) — C
THE BOOK OF DOLLY'S DOINGS by W. Copeland (Blackie) — C
THE BOOK OF DOLLY'S HOUSE by W. Copeland (Blackie) — C
THE BOOK OF DOLLY-LAND by W. Copeland (Blackie) — C
BOUNCING BABIES by W. Copeland (Blackie) — C
THE CHILD'S CHRISTMAS by E. Sharp (Blackie) — BW & C
FANCIFUL FOWLS by C. Robinson (Dent) — C
A LITTLE BOOK OF COURTESIES by K. Tynan (Dent) — BW
MAD MOTOR by W. Copeland (Blackie) — C
PECULIAR PIGGIES by C. Robinson (Dent) — C
ROAD, RAIL & SEA by C. Jerrold (Blackie) — BW & C
THE SILLY SUBMARINE by W. Copeland (Blackie) — C

1907
ALICE'S ADVENTURES IN WONDERLAND by L. Carroll (Cassell) — BW & C
BLACK BUNNIES by C. Robinson (Blackie) — C
BLACK DOGGIES by C. Robinson (Blackie) — C
BLACK SAMBOS by C. Robinson (Blackie) — C
THE CAKE SHOP by W. Copeland (Blackie) — C
PRINCE BABILLON by Nella (Sealey Clark) — BW
SONGS OF LOVE AND PRAISE by A. Matheson (Dent) — BW
THE STORY OF THE WEATHERCOCK by E. Sharp (Blackie) — BW & C
THE SWEET SHOP By W. Copeland (Blackie) — C
THE TOY SHOP by W. Copeland (Blackie) — C

BIBLIOGRAPHY

1908
BABES AND BLOSSOMS by W. Copeland (Blackie)	C
THE BOOK OF OTHER PEOPLE by W. Copeland (Blackie)	C
THE BOOK OF SAILORS by W. Copeland (Blackie)	C
THE BOOK OF SOLDIERS by W. Copeland (Blackie)	C
A CHILD'S GARDEN OF VERSES by R.L. Stevenson (Bodley Head)	BW & C
THE FAIRIES' FOUNTAIN by Countess E. Martinengo Cesaresco (Fairbairns)	BW & C
SONGS OF HAPPY CHILDHOOD by I. Maunder (Sealey Clark)	BW

1909
BABES AND BIRDS by J. Pope (Blackie)	C
THE VANISHING PRINCESS by N. Syrett (David Nutt)	BW

1910
BROWNIKINS AND OTHER FANCIES by R. Arkwright (Wells, Gardner, Darton)	BW & C
GRIMM'S FAIRY TALES (Ernest Lister)	BW & C
IN THE BEGINNING by S.B. Macy (Sealey Clark)	BW & C

1911
THE BABY SCOUTS by J. Pope (Blackie)	C
THE BIG BOOK OF FAIRY TALES by W. Jerrold (Blackie)	BW & C
THE SECRET GARDEN by F. Hodgson Burnett (Heinemann)	BW & C
THE SENSITIVE PLANT by P.B. Shelly (Heinemann)	BW & C

1912
BABES AND BEASTS by J. Pope (Blackie)	C
BEE: THE PRINCESS OF THE DWARFS by A. France (Dent)	C
THE BIG BOOK OF FABLES by W. Jerrold (Blackie)	BW & C
THE FOUR GARDENS by Handasyde (Heinemann)	BW & C
LONGFELLOW by M. MacLeod (Wells Gardner Darton)	BW & C
OLD TIME TALES edited by L. Marsh (Frowde Hodder Stoughton)	BW & C
SONGS OF INNOCENCE by W. Blake (Dent) Illustrated by Charles and Mary Robinson	BW & C

1913
A CHILD'S BOOK OF EMPIRE by A.T. Morris (Blackie)	BW & C
FAIRY TALES by C. Perrault (Dent)	BW & C
THE HAPPY PRINCE by O. Wilde (Duckworth)	BW & C
MARGARET'S BOOK by H. Fielding-Hall (Hutchinson)	BW & C
THE OPEN WINDOW by E.T. Thurston (Chapman & Hall)	BW
RAINBOWS by M. Dykes Spicer (Melrose)	BW
TOPSY TURVY by W.J. Minnion (The Connoisseur)	C

1914
OUR SENTIMENTAL GARDEN by A. & E. Castle (Heinemann)	BW & C

1915
ARABIAN NIGHTS: THE STORY OF PRINCE AHMED AND THE FAIRY PERIE BANOU (Gay & Hancock)	C
THE OPEN WINDOW by E.T. Thurston (Chapman & Hall)	BW & C

BIBLIOGRAPHY

RIP VAN WINKLE by W. Irving (T.C. & E.C. Jack) — BW & C
ROBERT HERRICK (Wells Gardner Darton) — BW & C
THE SONGS AND SONNETS OF WILLIAM SHAKESPEARE (Duckworth) — BW & C
WHAT HAPPENED AT CHRISTMAS by E. Sharp (Blackie) — BW & C

1919
BRIDGET'S FAIRIES by Mrs. S. Stevenson (Religious Tract Society) — BW & C

1920
SONGS OF HAPPY CHILDHOOD by I. Maunder (Sealey Clark) — BW
TEDDY'S YEAR WITH THE FAIRIES by M.E. Gullick (Religious Tract Society) — BW & C

1921
THE CHILDREN'S GARLAND OF VERSES by G. Rhys (Dent) — C
FATHER TIME STORIES by J.G. Stevenson (Religious Tract Society) — BW & C

1922
DORIS AND DAVID ALL ALONE by E. Marc (Hutchinson) — BW & C
THE GOLDFISH BOWL by P. Austin (Hutchinson) — BW & C

1923
WEE MEN by B. Girvin & M. Cosens (Hutchinson) — C

1925
ONCE ON A TIME by A.A. Milne (Hodder & Stoughton) — BW & C

1927
THE SAINT'S GARDEN by W. Radcliffe (S.P.C.K.) — BW

1928
MOTHER GOOSE NURSERY RHYMES (Collins) — BW & C
THE RUBAIYAT OF OMAR KHAYYAM (Collins) — C

1930
GRANNY'S BOOK OF FAIRY STORIES (Blackie) — BW & C

1932
YOUNG HOPEFUL by J. Dunbar (Jenkins) — BW

THE TRUE ANNALS OF FAIRYLAND:
THE REIGN OF KING HERLA 1900